ON THE COMMON

STORY OF A YOUNG BOY'S LIFE GROWING UP IN THE SAINTS

by
Terry Aldous

2011

First Edition

Published and Printed by

Leiston Press
Masterlord Industrial Estate
Leiston
Suffolk
IP16 4JD
Telephone Number: 01728 833003
Email: glenn@leistonpress.com

ISBN 978-1-907938-17-7

©Terry Aldous 2011

INTRODUCTION

Born during the war years, 11th April 1942 at the All Hallows
Hospital, Ditchingham. Middle child of mother Ellen and father
Harry. Brother Eric being the oldest and sister Daphne the
youngest. We were living in the village of St. Michael South
Elmham to give it its correct name. One of a group of villages all
ending South Elmham, St. James, St. Peter, St. Nicholas, St. Margaret
and so on. Bow and arrow land as it is commonly known,
without any mains water or electricity in the village at the time.
I will try to give an honest account of a young boy's life growing
up in the Saints until it was time to leave school at fifteen.

Terry Aldous

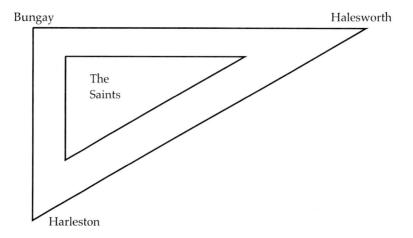

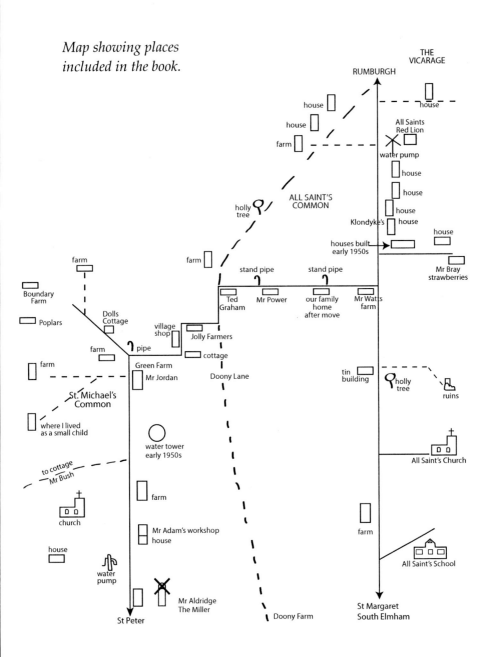

Map showing places included in the book.

The map opposite will give you a little idea where various people mentioned in the book lived. You will notice the water mill near The Red Lion and the stand pipes near our house. I think there were others on the common, one near Klondyke's house and another near the houses across the common. On the corner near Mr Watts Farm, The Willows, stood a war time shelter or Home Guard hut, it was something to do with war time activity as it had a blast wall in front of the door. What we used to call the tin buildings, these were actually cattle and implement sheds belonging to Mr Watts, now there is a property on the site. In the meadow opposite were ruins of an old house. Us boys used to take a few more bricks out now and again, we also used to tear the backside out of our trousers, sliding down the roof of the war time shelter.

As was the done thing, mother spent ten days in hospital when I came into the world. How we got home the 6 miles to St. Michaels I don't know, as in them days if you didn't ride a bike then you walked. As motor cars were very thin on the ground and mother was left to look after us as father was away at sea. Father used to tell the story that he didn't want to be a fisherman. On leaving school at 14 he wanted to work on a farm and got a job as cowman. He was busy with the afternoon milking. A cow kicked him and father being rather a quick-tempered man grabbed hold of the nearest broom and gave the cow a whack, unbeknown to father the farmer was watching proceedings over the cow shed door and with no more ado, father got the sack. With very little industry you either worked on the farms or went to sea. Somewhere in his early days he picked up the nickname of Sugar: Father was Old Sugar, as me and my brother got older, we were known as Big Sugar and Little Sugar. We rented the cottage at St. Michael off the neighbouring farmer. Thatched roof, big garden, a meat safe on the side of an outhouse, very small wire mesh front to keep the flies and insects out. I learned that it was also common to have a meat safe in the ground, a wooden box with a lid on. It was the forerunner of the 'modern day' fridge. I think mother used to do the garden with the help of a neighbour as we were always fed plenty of vegetables. I can remember a huge rhubarb patch, as we used to play hide and seek in it. Mother also had a big white cat, great big cat as big as a lion, but I suppose when you are small yourself everything seems big.

1

Most of all I remember we had a swing hanging from a branch of an apple tree. Me and my brother spent hours playing on that. There was a deep pond near the swing with some wooden steps going down to the water and that would be where mother fetched all the household water from. I would imagine she boiled the water for drinking I wouldn't know. There was a big hand pump up the other end of the village which would be too far to carry water home. As well as no mains water supply there was no electricity either. That didn't get to the villages, until my early teens 1953-54. All lighting was with paraffin lamps. The kind you see at the auctions nowadays making a fortune. Cooking was done in a big cast iron type cooking range which also provided winter warmth. In the summer time mother used a Valor cooking stove bottle of paraffin turned upside down on one end of the stove which would provide fuel for 2 burners to boil a kettle or whatever, and a small oven to cook in. After a winter of smoke and smuts from paraffin lamps and coal fires you can understand where the term spring clean came from.

The cottage is 500 yards from the road across the common, in the winter rubber wellies were everyday footwear. There was a fallen tree halfway across the common where me and my brother would sit under, eating a swede or white cabbage we had pulled up from the farmer's field. One of my earliest memories, I couldn't have been more than three because the war was still on; I was in the wicker child seat on the back of my mother's bicycle. She was walking beside the bike pushing it across the common on the way home, when all of a sudden mother picked me out of the seat, let go of the bike, laid me on the ground and laid on top of me, not pressing me into the dirt but covering me up. Out of the west over Green Farm came this aeroplane flying very low over me and mum, and disappearing into the east. No doubt she thought it was Jerry going to pop us off. Of course I wasn't old enough to know east or west then, but I remember it as clear as yesterday. I don't know where my brother was when this was going on. Perhaps my grandmother was at home looking after him (that's my mother's mother). Both my father's parents, and my mother's father died before I was born. Grandmother didn't appear to have a permanent home, she would stay with us a few months, then spend a few months with Aunt Alice (mother's older sister) before moving on elsewhere.

There must have been a P.O.W. camp somewhere in the area, as a dozen or so would be waiting to be picked up by this lorry with a canvas sheet over the back, dark green as I remember. They would wait on the corner near the letterbox. Some of them would be making corn dollies. I think they used to help on the local farms. I can't remember any guards but I suppose there must have been somebody otherwise they would have all cleared off.

Life was happy for a young lad growing up on St. Michael's common. Mother had a white rabbit in a hut behind the house. I expect it was called Snowy - all white rabbits are called Snowy. My brother Eric had started school and I was left to play and amuse myself on my own. There was no nursery school to go to, you went to school when you were five years old, the playing finished, learning started. Eleventh of April 1947 I reached the age of five and it was my turn to start school. The first day after the harvest holiday, smartly dressed in my short trousers, jacket and tie, I was off to school. Lucky for me my brother knew the ropes. We got on Lambert's big blue bus at the corner of St. Michael's common near the letterbox and off we went, picking up children in the villages of All Saints, St. James and St. Nicholas and arriving at All Saints school with half an hour to spare before lessons started. The school is still there to this day, it's a private dwelling. I think it ceased being a school in the 1960s.

3

My brother had me under his wing, holding hands near the school wall. I don't think I cried, feeling a bit subdued no doubt. This old lady came out of the school ringing a hand bell and we lined up ready to walk into school. The first thing I noticed when we got in the assemble / classroom was how high the windowsills were. I couldn't see out of the windows from down where I was, I could only see the sky. This is it I am on my own now, little ones lined up at the front, brother Eric being older was a couple of rows back. This old lady bell ringer, turned out to be the Head Mistress Mrs Ayers, she stood at the front of us all calling out our names, and when it got to your name you had to say "Yes miss!", (see learning already!). Next thing we were shown the toilets. You went out of the main building, across the yard to the urinals which were like a brick built shed with no door or roof on and you stood facing the inner wall. There was only one toilet for big jobs that did have a door on but had no flush, it was a bucket and chuck it type of toilet. The caretaker used to dig a hole and empty it at the rear of the premises.

After a few days at school it must have dawned on me that this was how it was going to be for a long time. I started to get unsettled for the next year or so. I led the teachers and no doubt my mum a merry dance. I started running home, the school bus would drop us off at school in the morning, I would be off and up the road, and slowly make my way home hiding in the hedge every time I saw somebody on a bike, because everybody in the village knew who should be at school. I got away with it for sometime, which unsettled my brother, so we both ran home. Mother and Mrs Ayers must have had to get together after a few weeks of that. There were no telephones so things took a lot longer to get sorted out. Any how, we duly arrived at school and getting ready to scarper, when Mrs Ayers stepped on the bus, took me and my brother by the scruff of the neck and marched us into her enclosed backyard behind the school house. Sat us down on

at school

Me and my brother at All Saints School.
He's holding me so I don't run home.

ALL SAINTS SCHOOL PHOTO
1951/52

Back row l-r: Clive Taylor, myself, Derek Copeman, our teacher Miss Bishop, Jean Watling and Tony Crockford

Third row l-r: Jane Taylor, Sam Cockrill, Mavis Collins, Jill Crockford, Albert Gillingwater and Aubrey Debenham

Second row l-r: Molly Copeman, Joy Pearce, Margaret Meadows, Faith Pearce, Pamela Pearce, Hope Pearce and Janet Warne

Front row l-r: person cut off I think is Jimmy Bush, ? Watling, Michael Collins, Desmond Flatt, Frank Walker, Henry Vincent. To the best of my knowledge the names are correct. The little girl looking looking over the teachers left shoulder unknown.

Brothers and sisters in the group: my cousins Clive and Jane Taylor, Derek and Molly Copeman, Michael and Mavis Collins, ? Watling and Jean Watling, Tony and Jill Crockford. Triplets in the group: Faith, Hope and Joy Pearce.

two small chairs, locked the door and that was us taken care of. I still used to nip off home at any given opportunity. It came to an end when I scarpered from school one dinner break. I was well down All Saints road near the white railings when I saw Mrs Ayers coming down the road on her bike hell for leather. I ran and hid behind a tree trunk. I then spotted my grandmother on her bike coming in the opposite direction. They met within earshot of me. Voices were raised and what they were going to do with me when they caught me, don't bear thinking about. Skinning alive was mentioned. I stood up, the game was over. I must have realised this couldn't go on forever. I didn't run home anymore.

Our home at St. Michaels was one of a terrace of three, the end one, left side looking from the front. A big event was about to happen in our lives; mother and father had bought a house in the next village. Haylocks Cottage, All Saints. Father had some time home from sea and we moved house with a horse and tumbrel borrowed from Mr Jordan across the common. I can remember it very well. Me and my brother riding in the tumbrel, father leading the horse. We made several journeys to and fro, no more than a mile each way, passing Mrs Head's village shop and St Michael's Jolly Farmers on the way. The shop closed in the 1950s and the Jolly Farmers in the 1960s. The horse's name was Scott, a Suffolk Punch, a steady old horse getting on in years, not very tall. As with all farmers, Mr Jordan had a few horses and no doubt thought Scott was right for the job.

At the end of the day the family and all the possessions were at Haylocks Cottage, a two up two down pebble dashed, thatched, detached cottage, vegetable garden to the left. Two apple trees, a plum tree as well, and a pond to the right, flower garden at the front, with a lovely pink rose climbing up the front of the house. Mother decided she wanted another linen line. So before father

7

went back to sea she sent him down Doony Lane to cut two posts out of the hedge. Holes were dug and the post put in either end of the garden with a piece of twine in-between. It wasn't long before the post started to sprout leaves and branches, mother had a willow tree at each end of the linen line. Still no mains water or electricity. There was a public house in the village; All Saints Red Lion. Landlady was Mrs Baldry. All looking out over All Saints common with two big ponds, one deep surrounded with trees and bushes, the other shallow and open. In the middle of the common there was this tree shaped like a Christmas tree. That put my young mind at rest. At least we will have a Christmas tree. (It turned out to be a hawthorn.) We still went to the same school. It was on the same route. We hadn't been living there long before sister Daphne came into the world. Mother had a big grey Marmit pram and I used to push my sister miles in that. I don't know how I saw where I was going as they are big tall machines. The roads were very safe, if you saw a car it was a talking point. The biggest fear was the cows, all the farmers in the village had grazing rights. All the cows would graze together and wander all over the place. I wasn't afraid of all the cows but there was one black and white cow which used to wear a mask. We used to call her Tin Face. She would put her head up and give chase. It was ok if she was on the common, but if we came across her near the road we wouldn't go past. It was great fun exploring our new surroundings. Spending hours playing down Doony Lane, or Unce's Lane as we used to call it. My Uncle Jack and Aunt Alice used to live down the bottom of the lane, along with their two children Dolly and Herbert. They had a small holding down there keeping a few animals including a house cow, and growing wheat, barley and potatoes. The nearest road was at least a mile away, but there's nothing left of the house and building now, only the odd bit of brick rubble if you know where to look. Uncle Jack and Aunt Alice are long gone. Doony Lane was another world for a young lad. Trees to

8

climb, places to hide, play Cowboys and Indians, making pop guns out of Elder wood, using acorns for bullets, fishing in the pond. Soon sorted a fishing rod out of a piece of stick, garden twine, bent pin, dig up a worm and we went fishing.

Mother was getting the house in order. New thatch on the roof, new Sofono cooking range in the kitchen. Brother Eric being a bit older than me was taking an interest in the vegetable plot. Still no mains electric or water, although we have moved on from pond water. Near the Red Lion there was a windmill which pumped water to two overhead tanks which was piped to taps around the village, one of which was not far from our house. A regular job for me or my brother was to fetch a couple of buckets of water each day. Then there was also the well in the garden where we had a bucket on the end of a piece of rope which we used to lower down the well and pull up a bucket of water, that was harder than carrying a bucket full from the tap. Everyday a tradesman would call; butcher, baker, milkman, greengrocer, hardware (he was very important as he sold paraffin for the lamps and the Valor cooker). Every Tuesday Mr Emery from Bungay would bring the accumulator for the radio and take the other one away for charging up. The radio was our only form of entertainment. I used to like listening to boxing. Don Cockell, Randolf Turpin, Rocky Marciano were my heroes. Life seemed a bit more orderly in them days. Without fail we always had a joint of beef for sunday dinner (midday), mashed potatoes, gravy and veg. There would always be some meat left over to have cold for Monday with a few potatoes and whatever. Because Monday was wash day it was an all day affair and not a lot of time for making dinner; there would be water boiling everywhere. That would be a slow process, from handwashing to the mangle and then on to the linen line. It went on into the evening. There would be a day for ironing, another performance. You had to have your fire alight, otherwise you couldn't heat your irons up. I have still got two of them old irons in my shed now, my wife used to use them when we first got married. Baking day, that was a weekly event; cannot remember what day that was. We used to get off the school bus at the end of the day and chase off home. Mother would be up to her elbows in flour, surrounded by wonderful homemade fruit cake, jam tarts, old maids, sausage rolls, all sorts of goodies, nobody worried about the fat contents. If you carried a bit of weight you were seen as being fat and healthy. Mother was a great cook. Could knock up anything. She learned to cook in service, as a single girl. She worked downstairs, in the big house, as it was termed, somewhere in the Bungay area. After the baking was finished there was the usual squabble for who was going to have the rest of the mixture in the mixing bowls.

There was a bus service from the village. Lamberts used to run a bus to Bungay every Thursday afternoon which allowed people in the villages a chance to do some shopping. In later years Naylor from Halesworth used to run a bus to Harleston, also Eastern Counties started a regular service into Halesworth and Southwold. Mother used to take us to the seaside at Southwold on the bus which was a great day out. Especially if it was a double decker bus, we would sit at the front and see for miles. Before we caught the bus to come home we would always go the the Dutch Barn Restaurant for a cup of tea and a bun, it's still there today.

One thing that really sticks out in my mind was the cold winters we had, and the snow. The ponds were frozen over with thick ice. All the children in the village would be sliding on the ice, building snow men and having a whale of a time. One winter we didn't go to school for two weeks as there was that much snow. The bus couldn't get through. Farmers had to pour milk down the drain as the lorry couldn't get through to collect the milk churns. The local farmers had the job of keeping the roads clear as best they could with a snow plough. A 'V' shaped contraption would be dragged along the road behind a tractor with a man trying to keep it straight with a pair of handles at the back. Us children had great fun walking in the maiden snow where it had blown into drifts making lovely patterns through the hedges. Often you would fall through up to your neck in snow where it had drifted over a ditch. Sand was used to grit the roads. Each village had its sand heap. They are still evident today after the snow has cleared. Sand would be spread manually on corners and hills, and no doubt the council replenished the sand heaps. Us children used to play in the sand, digging holes and making sand castles. Whilst we are on about sand, another great spectacle we used to like watching was the tar pot. During the summer, lorries would cart sand to leave heaps both sides of the road for miles. Then the steam roller would turn up. Together with the tar spreading machine and the living quarters (as some of the road gang would only go home at weekends if they didn't live local). The tar would be spread on the road. The road gang would spread the sand on top and the roller would chug backwards and forwards rolling it down. We used to love watching that. The old engine hissing and spitting. We used to get dabbed up with tar. Mother wasn't very happy about that. Stop/Go boards or traffic lights were not in existence. Apart from the milk lorry, tradesman vans and the odd car, that's all there was to stop proceedings.

A Mr Tinny Day from Metfield used to run a contracting business ploughing with steam engines. One engine stationed at each end of the field, dragging the plough across the field from one machine to the other with a big wire rope. A man would be on the plough keeping it straight with a big steering wheel. I also watched them doing a pond out with a steam engine either side of the pond dragging a big old bucket affair across and dumping the mud round the edge of the pond. The men operating these machines would also sleep and live in the living quarters which would be on site and no doubt visit the Jolly Farmers or The Red Lion in the evening.

As you can gather, me, my brother and sister had started to wander off. My sister used to play with the girls from across the common, playing what young girls play. My brother got himself a job at the farm down the road. He worked after school and weekends looking after chickens. He was paid sixpence per hour. Two and a half pence in today's values. I wasn't interested in earning a bob at that stage. If I heard a tractor working the fields in the distance, then I was off to find it. It would be either Cliffy Holland tractor driver for Mr Horace Watts at Willows Farm or Roy Jordan who worked for his father at Green Farm, St Michael Willows Farm being in All Saints.

They would see me coming across the fields, short trousers and rubber boots, stop the tractor, I would climb up and sit on the mudguard and ride up and down the field for ages. To a lad knee high to a grasshopper the tractors seemed huge. They were E27N Fordson Majors. As well as tractors there were still a lot of horses on the farms then. I had a lucky escape involving horses. On one of my forays down Doony Lane I came across Roy Jordan muck carting. He was carting from the muck heap to the field putting muck on to small heaps across the field in rows ready to be spread. This was done by the farm workers using four Tyne forks. Any how, Roy was using two horses one in the shafts of the tumbril and a horse in front with chains coming from its collar to the shafts (it was called using a trace horse). I wanted a ride, so Roy put me on the front horse, big old Suffolk Punch a long way up. 'Giddy up!', the horses moved to the next heap, 'woo!' they stopped. 'Giddy up!', I wasn't holding on tight enough and I fell off with eight big old feet and two tumbril wheels about to go over me; Roy grabbed me from the ground with a, "are you alright boy?". Dusted me down, I thought I had better keep on the ground and walk. Then I heard the whistle. My mother acquired a whistle from somewhere and at meal times mother would blow the whistle. On a still day you could hear it for miles. If we didn't hear it someone did. Your mother is blowing they would say, and we would head for home. At the northern end of the village of St Michael was a windmill, there is still a property there today, but the mill is long gone. The last person to operate the windmill was Mr Aldrich. Mr Aldrich the miller as he was known locally. You will see today in St Michael's churchyard, inside the gate on the right a headstone on Mr Aldrich's grave with a windmill carved on it. At the weekends he would be seen out on his rounds with his horse and tumbril, pulling a three wheeled water cart. The lid of the water cart was like two half doors closing on top of it. Also a big tap at the back. He would stop at the stand pipe near our house, uncouple the water cart and put a piece of hosepipe from the stand pipe to the cart, turn the tap on and give me or my brother a penny or two to turn the tap off when the cart was full of water. In the meantime he would carry on, tumbril piled high with sacks of meal he had ground the week previous, delivering to farms in Rumburgh, All Saints and St James, and collect grain to grind the next week, if the wind blew. At this time tractors were getting a bit more advanced, some had a pulley wheel where you could attach a belt and with more livestock being kept they couldn't rely on the wind to blow to feed them, so a grinder was purchased and stood inside the barn. A belt from the tractor would turn the grinder and the farmer was able to produce his own meal, which was the beginning of the end for such people as Mr Aldrich the miller. He would couple up the water cart and drag home with him on his way back. About this time there was some sadness in the family. I got up one morning and my Uncle Billy was being consoled by my mother. He was crying and very upset. His wife my Aunt Doreen had died. I wasn't really old enough to take it all in. But they had already suffered the loss of a daughter Topsy aged just 4 years. My Aunt Doreen was just 29

13

years when she died, leaving my uncle and five children, my cousins; I can remember the day of the funeral. My Mother told me to go and play down Doony Lane. Off I went and came across Roy Jordan and some more fellows, chopping out sugar beet so I went over to them. I looked towards the road and I had never seen so many motor cars heading for St Michael's church before. My Aunt Doreen was buried near her daughter Topsy, and has recently been joined by my Uncle Billy (Taylor). I expect my brother went off somewhere, and my sister went with mother as she was only a babe in arms. It was about this time that one Sunday morning I was carrying my sister downstairs and I dropped her. She landed at the bottom, screaming and crying. Mother appeared, sent me off across the common to ask Mr Bealings if he could take mother and my sister to Ditchingham Hospital. He had a car and done a bit of taxi work. Off they went, I was some worried, not so much about what I had done to my sister, more about what's going to happen to me when they get back. They were gone hours. It was the middle of the afternoon when they got back. I was worried even more when I saw mother carrying sister out of the car, her right arm was set in plaster as stiff as a board. "Terence" mother said "your sister has broken her arm". When I had done something wrong it was always a stern Terence! All other times it was Terry. But mother being the good mother she was, didn't take it any further.

My older brother was spending more time working at Willows Farm. He kept a book upstairs on the bedside wash table where he would write down his hours and amount he was paid. I got to thinking perhaps its time I started earning a bob or two, so I had the idea that if I round up the cows on the common at milking time and drive them home to their respective farms, the farmer might give me a bob for saving his time. But that didn't work, only one farmer ever gave me anything and that you could put in your eye. So then started my life long love of livestock. I know what to do I will keep some rabbits and sell the young ones in Halesworth market. Mother encouraged this idea as she already had some hens in the yard and she liked animals. You will have to make some huts mother said. We had an old cast iron wall oven in the yard, if I drill some holes in the front of that I can then fix a wire netting frame on. So off I go to a family in St Michael who I know have a drill they might lend me. As happy as Larry I returned with the drill, got down to business of drilling some holes in this oven. I turned, I turned and I turned, the drill made no impression whatsoever, so I gave up on that idea. Out came the wood saw, hammer and nails, and found some material somewhere, with that knocked up some rabbits' huts. I have always to this day been a dab hand at rough carpentry. It was no trouble getting some rabbits. To start with everybody in the village kept rabbits. Little rabbits quickly grew into big rabbits. Mother had an interest in this and informed me one of my rabbits wants to be a mother and I was to put the rabbit in a sack and take it to Mr Howlett in St Margaret's who had a buck rabbit. Leave it with me young man he said, come and collect it tomorrow evening and bring two shillings with you. That was his fee for the use of his buck rabbit. Next evening I went and collected my rabbit. He informed me that all being well she will have some young ones in a months time. From there my rabbit empire grew. Mother's old Marmit pram had been put to good use as a go cart and was still parked up in the yard. So armed with a tin of paint and a brush I painted 'Terry Aldous Rabbit Breeder' on both sides of the pram. I kept four sacks in the pram. I would fill them all up with hog weed from the hedgerow and road side, put them in the pram and push it home. It wasn't long before I was putting rabbits into a box and taking them to

Halesworth market. They would make one shilling to two shillings each at eight weeks old. I had an empty hut and for one reason or another I biked over to Mr Benny Fullers at Flixton to see if he would sell me a pair of pigeons. I can't remember where the bike came from or ever learning to ride. Benny was in the barn. Yes he said go and catch a pair in that building over there, they will cost you two bob. Keep them shut in for a couple of weeks and they should be alright. I was a bit worried about them being cold in my hut. Mother had an aluminium hot water bottle, so I filled that up with water from the kettle on the fire to keep them warm. After two weeks I let them out, they flew from the hut to the roof of the house and it wasn't long before they were gone. On my bike off to Benny Fullers. Yes, the pigeons got there just before I did. This routine went on a few times till I got fed up with that. With an ever increasing rabbit population the hut was soon in use. Toby and Smokey came on the scene. My desk mate at school told me that the farm up the road have some kittens they want to give away. So rather than go home on the school bus I went up the farm and got two kittens and carried them home in a box. Mother wasn't at all pleased "Don't you think you have enough now to look after." she said. But I managed to convince mother they would be better off with us. They were both long haired kittens. Smokey was the weaker one of the two and he or she died after a week or so. But Toby made a lovely cat and lived to be twenty years old. Mother would have been more agreeable to having the kittens but she had already bought a black labrador bitch puppy from Mr Watts at Willows Farm. Linda we named her. She lived in a kennel under the apple tree just outside the back door. I have two reasons for remembering Linda, one good, one bad. I will deal with the bad one first. Mother had a pond in the back yard, quite deep, it was probably a borrow pit dug out for clay to build the house, as it was and still is clay lump. There was some concrete steps down to the waters edge. I was playing with Linda, she jumped up and knocked me down the steps. I was under water thrashing about in a panic and my whole young

Father at time of getting his Mates Ticket

Father went to sea from the age of fourteen to his retirement at
seventy. Steam drifters, herring catching, long lining to diesel
trawlers and finished up on rig watch vessels. Old Sugar was a
well known figure around his home port of Lowestoft. He sailed
in various boats, Patria, Silver Crest, Feaco, Marshal Pak etc. The
pictures show father in different ports, dress and modes around
the country.

In all his fishing clothing

17

At Milford Haven

Father aboard ship

Father in happy mode

Father with the fish

Father and shipmates

Mother outside our house on St Michael common
(notice the tree where the swing was on)

Like a lot of single young ladies, Mother went into service. The family think it was Earsham Hall near Bungay. The unknown lady in the photo *(on the next page)* was probably head of the household, she looks rather stearn.

In the doorway of our home at St Michael's *(above)*, Mum as I have always remembered her; in her trademark pinefore!

Mother's white cat

Mother in service as a young lady
(other person unknown)

Mother before the family came along

Mum & Dad - courting days

Mum and my sister at the seaside

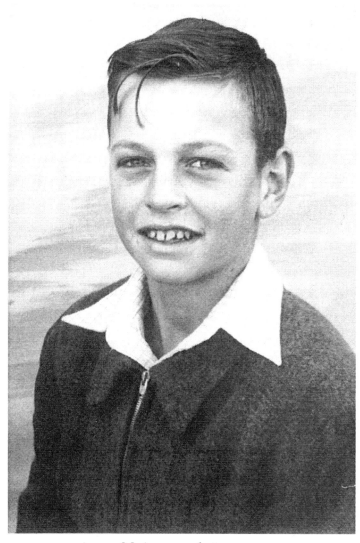

Me in my early teens
(notice a chipped tooth caused messing about with my brother)

**With my brother and sister at various stages of childhood.
Short trousers was the order of the day!**

Me and my brother 1946–47
I can remember going to Bungay to
sit for this photograph.
Great big box camera on a tripod.

Must have been our first photo
I was probably 3 years old

A trip to the seaside.
The only photograph with
my brother and sister on.

life passed before me. I was saying goodbye to mum, dad, brother and sister. I thought I was going to meet my maker. But thank the Lord I grabbed a piece of wood at the bottom of the steps. I pulled myself out gasping for air coughing and crying. That was the nearest I have ever got to being a gonner! The good memory of Linda was when she had a litter of pups. It all started when I was taking Linda for a walk on a lead. I was near Willows Farm when Jock came out, a big black labrador dog. Well I didn't really understand what was going on. I hadn't seen that sought of behaviour before, not even with my rabbits, I wasn't allowed to. I dropped the lead, left Linda with Jock and ran home to tell mother. She said go back and throw a bucket of water over them, that didn't seem to make a lot of difference, so I left them alone. Linda came home when she was ready and of course nine weeks later she had a litter of pups, I think she had five. They were a lot of fun. When they were old enough we used to race them up the road. One of us would hold Linda on the road outside the house and we would take the puppies to the end of the road and let them go having a pretend bet on which one would get back first. We had them till they were eight weeks old and mother had to sell them. They got up to no good. Mr Watts had some cockerels in the orchard at the back of the house. Going outside one morning we noticed a trail of feathers from the shed where the pups slept, up the ditch and into the orchard and they had killed half a dozen cockerels. Poor mother had to go and tell Mr Watts. The puppies were soon gone to new homes after that.

There was the Queen's Coronation about this time. Everybody in the village was invited to a party on the green in front of All Saints school. All the tables and chairs were put out in rows draped with tablecloths. We all had our fill. After the party there were running races and sack races for children and adults, we all had a whale of a time. Flixton races was an annual event. I don't know why it was called Flixton races because all the tents and start and finish line was in a meadow north of the 'S' bends which

I believe is St Margaret's Ilketshall. There were jumps erected in the ditches and the course went behind what is now St Peter's Brewery, across the fields to Mr Legrice's land which was in Flixton and back in front of St Peter's Brewery on to the finish in the meadow at the 'S' bends. It was quite a big oval circuit. I used to bike there after school, have a Parravani ice cream and watch these great big horses galloping by. When you are only knee high to a grasshopper everything seems big. I suppose it's what today they call a point to point race meeting. Also in the summer months mother used to take us out quite a bit. She liked agricultural shows. We went to the Suffolk and Norfolk shows, probably not both in the same year. I can only remember going to Costessey near Norwich for the Norfolk Show, but I think it used to move around the county like the Suffolk Show as I can remember going to Benacre Park amongst the conker trees in the early 1950s to the Suffolk Show. At the Suffolk Show there were these two blue tractors linked up, the front of the rear tractor coupled up to the rear of the front tractor and the front tractor had no wheels at the front. What a sight for small eyes that was! It, or that was going round and round over a great mound of soil. I have since learned that the tractor was Ernest Doe's Triple D Two Fordson Majors joined up. As children still do today we used to sit on the tractors pretending to be tractor drivers. They were mostly Grey Fergusons, Fordson Majors, David Browns and my favourite, I used to call the 'Pom Pom Tractor' the Field Marshall. If I hear one today it still gets my attention. The poultry and rabbit tents were of interest to me. All different types and colours of rabbits. Different to what I had at home! Mine were all multi colours. Of particular interest to me were the names and addresses on the carrying boxes under the pens. One I remember came from Blackpool. Very much later in life I came to know the man. Mother's highlight of the shows were the flower tent. The roses, mother loved roses; Peace, Enna, Harkness etc. Haylocks Cottage, All Saints was adorned with

24

roses. There is a rose on mother's headstone in St Michael's churchyard.

We had a trip to Ipswich. I was not keen on going in and out of shops. The one thing about the Ipswich trip I remember were the trams everywhere. Tracks in the road, cables above the street and these trams with two arms on the roof touching the cables. I think Lowestoft also had trams as mother took us to see the carnival and I can remember the tracks in the road there. What a lovely day out that was! The noise, music and the colour I had never seen anything like that before. A trip to Yarmouth I remember for a different reason. I must have sent my mother up the wall. We walked down the arcade and on the corner we came across a pet shop. There were some puppies in the window. I wanted one. "You are not taking one of them home" said mother, "we have enough in the yard now with Linda, Toby and all the rabbits." Also my brother was getting interested in chickens. I started crying. We went in a restaurant for dinner, I was still crying - I want a puppy. I thought at one time mother was weakening. But no such luck I didn't get to take a puppy home. Poor mother took us children for a day out and I spent my time putting on my parts and crying. What we did bring home from Yarmouth were a couple of yachts to sail on the pond. Me and my brother got up early next morning and took these yachts with us and for one reason or another went and saw our Aunt Alice down Doony Lane. We told her mother knows where we are, she didn't. We played about down there to well into the afternoon, and we spotted father who was home from sea at the time coming down the lane looking for us. We knew he would be angry as we went off with these yachts telling nobody. Mother must have been worried sick. It was time for me and my brother to make a run for it. So we took a detour across the fields. Father spotted us and gave chase. We headed for home and got there before he did. And we climbed up onto the chickens hut out of his way. It wasn't long before father arrived on the scene. Being a short man he couldn't reach us, so he went into the shed and came out carrying a bag of potatoes and he set about pelting us with these potatoes. Some were hitting some were missing. The majority ended up in the pond, other side of the hen house. A much relieved mother came to our rescue and got on to father for throwing all the spuds in the pond. We came down off the hen house and were sent to our bedroom until things calmed down. Can't remember what happened to the yachts, I expect she put them out of our way somewhere. They caused her enough worry as it was.

Lincolnshire tulip fields is another trip we used to go on. Most of these excursions were with Lamberts coaches when they were based in Ditchingham. They used to run from Bungay Buttercross. We would get to Bungay by taxi either Mr Bealings from All Saints common or Mr Preston from Ditchingham. I can only remember one school trip. That was when I was at All Saints school. We went on a train journey. You couldn't do it today as it's all gone. We caught the train at Bungay and went through Homersfield, Harleston and on to Pulham. I think I am right in saying that the railway line ran roughly where the Bungay to Harleston main road is and Bungay station opposite side of the road to where the golf club now is. I don't think Bungay Golf Club was on the common as it was all let out to local farmers to graze cattle and horses on. Mr Jordan at St Michael's used to graze horses and foals on Bungay Common in the summer months. Usually from April to October. His horses were Suffolk Punches. When it was time to bring them home to the farm they used to walk them home, Mr Jordan and his sons. I went along to join in the fun of walking half a dozen horses through the streets of Bungay up St Margaret's Hill, all the way home to St Michael's. Sometime walking used to turn into a gallop but nevertheless they all used to get home. The young horses would then be broken in to work. First they would have a halter put on them and tied to a post in the horse yard. At first they would buck and rear up and go round and round in circles. After half a day of that they would tire and stand all hang dog looking. Then they would get used to the harness bit by bit. The bridle, then the collar, followed by the saddle and breeches. This would take a few weeks and finally the day would arrive when the horse was to be put in the cart. This was usually a Sunday morning activity so not to interfere with other weekday work I suppose. But I was glad it was weekends as I was able to watch. By now the horse had got used to having the harness on. It was led out of the stable all harnessed up, out on to the meadow where there would be a tumbril with its shafts up in the air taken there by one of the older horses. Roy Jordan would get in the tumbril, his brothers or father Jack would position the horse with a lot of 'woo' and 'steady', under the shafts and very steadily lower the shafts down over the saddle so the horse had got the weight of the tumbril. One would hold the horse's head whilst the other coupled up the collar, breeches and the belly gat under the horse to stop the tumbril kicking up again. Once that was done they would fix a long rein to the horse's bridle, hand it to Roy in the cart and get out of the way. I was watching all this at a good distance. Roy would say 'gee up!'. Nothing would happen so he would give it a little flick of the rein. The horse would move for the first time in a cart, the wheels would start clattering, the horse would take fright and they would take flight. Roy holding on for dear life. Talk about chariots of fire! Round the meadow they went at full pelt. The harder the horse went the more the tumbril rattled. They went past me in a flash. Through the gate, across the next meadow and out of sight. They had gone for some time before they came back. The horse walking slowly in the tumbril completely exhausted, and Roy standing up in the back. The horse would be introduced to the tumbril several more times before being put to work proper. The next stage of this horse's learning was being put to plough. I remember the young horse being coupled up to Scott. The same horse father borrowed to move us from St Michael to All Saints. Both horses had chains from their collars to the yoke on the plough. Scott being the older and wiser of the two, set off at a steady pace and the young horse trying to drag old Scott and the plough along, trying to get it all done in five minutes. It didn't take many trips up and down the field before it realised it was doing all the work and both horses were in step walking together. One in the furrow and the other on the top. I can remember all this as I used to walk beside them with my rubber boots on and my little old legs used to be chapped where the rubber boots chafed. I was lucky enough to be growing up in the period that horses were still used on farms. Cutting hay with the clipper, turning, drag raking, carting it to the stack yard. Young boys and girls were put to good use on farms in them days. Feeding the hens, collecting eggs, hunting for nests because the barnyard fowl used to lay anywhere. Driving away at harvest and haysle time which entailed leading the horse and cart loaded from the field to the stack yard and taking the empty horse and cart back, usually two horses and carts on the go. Also harvest provided a bit of entertainment for those with the time. After the corners were mown out the binder would start cutting the corn spitting out the sheaths ready to be stood on end into shocks. The binder would be either pulled by two horses or a tractor going round and round working towards the middle. Rabbits would be looking to make a run for it as the piece of standing corn got smaller and smaller. Villagers would turn up armed with a stick and a dog, position themselves around the remainder of the corn and the rabbits made a break for it. With luck there would be one or two for the pot! In the holidays and after school I used to help with chopping out sugar beet, all done with a garden hoe. Dudley Jordan used to say to me hoe on my row and you can come home with me to dinner. Dinner time arrived and I went in the wash house with Dudley, washed my hands and went and sat at the table, Dudley sat at one end. His wife Kathy dished out the dinner, Kathy was looking very cross and not a word was spoken and I noticed it was only me and Dudley who were eating. I wasn't very old and didn't think too much about it. I had a lovely meal, but he never asked me to hoe on his row again and as I got older and thought about it I suppose it was a day when she was a bit short but mustered up a meal for herself and Dudley, he invited me round and she had no choice but to give me her dinner. I reckon he got an ear bashing when he went in for tea. I can remember another event involving Dudley with his father Jack and brothers Roy and John, they were thatching the corn stacks. I was feeling thirsty so I was helping myself to his bottle of lemonade. Unbeknown to me he was watching me, and asked me to go and ask Roy's wife Muriel the time. I came back, told him the time, carried on whatever I was doing. After a while I thought I would have another swig of lemonade, but I noticed the bottle was full. They were all falling about laughing. You can guess what the bottle was topped up with! But it learnt me a lesson.

In the early to mid fifties farmers were being encouraged to grow bigger and better crops. Hedges were being pulled out. Ponds and ditches filled in to grow more food to feed the nation. A firm named Blast That Stump were kept busy in the area blowing out the tree stumps. They would turn up in their van with all the necessary equipment. They would dig out around the tree stump, pack it with dynamite. I don't know whether they lit a fuse or ran an electric charge to it. I never got close enough to find out. After they had finished blasting you never saw such a mess. Tree stumps and roots from one side of the field to the other leaving

29

great big craters in the ground. The debris would be put on a big heap for burning. A bulldozer would turn up to fill the craters and the ditch in and what was two small fields is now one big one which meant you lost all the small fields. The three acres called the three corned field for obvious reasons, Jolly field because it was close to St Michael's Jolly Farmers. The Wine so called because looking at it from Doony Lane the field was on the wine or on the huh, it didn't have a straight side to it. Long Meadow, fifty yard wide and about five hundred yards long. The Spong, another meadow surrounded with blackberry bushes which in the season a lot of people in the village went blackberry picking. Picking extraordinary amounts to supplement their income. Mrs Baldry at All Saints Red Lion would take them off you and pay something like 9d to a shilling per pound and she would sell them on to Mr Percy Savage who would ply his trade on Monday of each week selling meat and fish also other bits and pieces from his van and no doubt he had an outlet for blackberries. These meadows at sometime had horses grazing on them which encouraged the growth of mushrooms, great big things as big as dinner plates. Apart from blackberry bushes there was an abundance of oak trees in the hedges around the fields. A lot of them were sold to Watts Timber Merchants in Bungay which no longer exists. There was a garden centre on the old wood yard site but that has since moved to Flixton Road Bungay. The tree felling gang would turn up in great big lorries, pulling a trailer - timber drugs we used to call them. I can't remember hearing the noise of chain saws, I think they were felled and cut up by hand. Loading the great big tree trunks on to the trailer was a grand site for a young boy's eyes. The trailer would be disconnected from the timber drug (lorry). The logs would be dragged to the trailer and laid length ways alongside the trailer. Two big wooden ramps would be attached, one end to the trailer, the other on the ground. Wire ropes would be attached to the timber drug on the opposite side of the trailer. Under and over the tree trunk and the loose end attached back to the timber drug and it would pull these tree trunks up the ramps onto the trailer, and what a site to behold. These huge big timber drugs loaded up with tree trunks. Engines roaring, black smoke belching out of the exhaust pipes as they struggle out of water logged fields, wheels spinning and skidding in the mud making for the road.

My first time driving a tractor on my own I will always remember. I thought all my Christmases had come at once! One Saturday morning Roy Jordan said to me Young Sugar I will set you off cultivating a field down Doony Lane. The tractor was a Fordson E27N and the cultivator was one where you pulled a cord at the end of the field, you would turn round pull the cord and the cultivator would go back in the ground again. Roy said I have set the throttle, no need to touch it you will be going plenty fast enough. So off I went, Roy went back to the farm and I was tractor driving on my own. Look at me I am a big boy now. I was over the moon. As the morning wore on I got to thinking about what am I going to do at dinner time. Mother do the dinner for twelve o'clock, she will be out blowing the whistle. I can't stop the tractor because it didn't have a self starter. You had to swing the handle at the front and I wasn't strong enough to do that. I will have to leave it ticking over and hope it won't stop. I counted the teeth on the throttle to where Roy had set it, left it on tick over and off I went for dinner. Haylocks Cottage was about a mile away so I wouldn't have heard the tractor running. After a hurried dinner I made my way back up Doony Lane and I was mighty pleased when I first saw puffs of smoke coming out of the exhaust pipe and as I got nearer I could hear the tractor was still running. Climbed on to the seat, reset the throttle and I was cultivating all afternoon.

By now I had taken the eleven plus exam and started at the Bungay County Modern School. Still got on the school bus on the corner of All Saints common at about eight o'clock in the morning. Picking up children at St James, St Nicholas and dropping juniors off at All Saints School, onto St Margaret's South Elmham, St Cross and dropping off at Flixton School. At Flixton quite a few of us got off the bus and played about in the woods until the bus came back. As it used to go on to Homersfield, pick more children up and come back to Flixton School where the juniors would get off and the rest of us would get back on and arrived at Bungay School just before nine o'clock.

The school was E shaped. Girls entrance on the right, boys on the left, with the offices and assembly hall in the middle and gardens filled the areas in between. It was a good school for teaching the basics, needlework and cookery for the girls, gardening, woodwork and metal work for the boys. I was quite good at woodwork. I suppose all the rabbit hut building stood me in good stead. No need to ask what I built in woodwork classes. It was a real modern, double hut with double doors at the front and sliding door access at both ends of course when it was finished I had to get it home. I couldn't afford transport so I borrowed the schools four wheeled trolley and dragged it all the way home to All Saints, up St Margaret's Hill and a few more hills along the way, and next morning drag the trolley all the way back, thankfully empty. My brother also made a rabbit hut and a kennel for Linda. He was also handy with a piece of wood. Dancing and music was low on my list of priorities, although I do like music. We had a school song, set to the tune of the Archers on the radio it went -

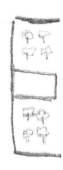

We are the county modern school
We are the county scholars
Girls in frocks so neat and smart
Boys in nice clean collars
Never sappy
Always happy, is the golden rule
Why not come and join the fun
We have at Bungay School.

Our backyard at home was still full of livestock. I had my rabbits, brother Eric has now got some chickens Curtiss and Aldrich were calling each Monday to buy the eggs from him. Not to be out done I sent away for eight 8 week old black leg horn pullets. I knocked up a hut and chicken run amongst the currant bushes in the corner of the garden. Got on my bike and cycled to Halesworth railway station and told them that I am expecting some livestock and would they phone Mr Power at the White House and he will collect them for me. I was looking forward to the chickens arriving and used to get off the school bus and run home. "Have the chickens come mum?" "No not yet!" After about three days and still no chickens, excitement turned to worry. Where are they? Are they at the railway station and they haven't phoned Mr Power. Will they be dead in the box? Have they got any food or water? I was getting in a right old state. It must have been a weekend as I was at home in the garden and Mr Power pulled up in his car. I have just had a call from Halesworth station, they have a box of livestock for you. I felt a mixture of excitement, are they alive or are they dead? Half an hour past and Mr Power pulled up outside the house and handed me the box. "I think they are alive," he said. Up the garden I went and opened the box and there were eight healthy black leghorn pullets. They were glad of a bit of freedom and I was pleased to see them. After harvest I went and asked Mr Watts at the Willows Farm if I could put my chickens on the shack. He didn't have any objection so I moved the chickens' hut to the middle of a field of wheat stubble where they would live off corn that dropped to the ground before and during harvest. It was a common site to see chicken huts out on corn fields after harvest. Roy Jordan's hut you could see for miles around. It was a great big shepherds hut he bought at a local auction. When he first got it home his wife Muriel said "what are you going to keep in that elephants"! You would also see pigs out on the bean stubble. They would all be back home after a month or so of gleaning the fields.

We are now into the mid fifties, 1954-55. Pipes were being left in heaps around the village of All Saints. They are laying the water on. Mother got the local builder in. He constructed a unit with a big stone sink, draining board and cupboards underneath. By that time the pipes were laid and each property had their own stop cock. The builder ran a pipe to the tap above the new sink and we had mains running water. The water mill outside the Red Lion which had supplied water for the village for years was made redundant and soon dismantled and gone forever. Not long after, the water was laid on, the electricity poles appeared. Gangs of men digging holes, followed by another gang putting the poles in, swinging up the poles putting the tee piece on and wiring up. Mother had the house wired up and we had electric light which was followed by a three legged galvanised Burco boiler and a small cooker. No more paraffin lamps or cookers and black ceilings. But light and cooking at the flick of a switch, I think an electric radio soon appeared with the battery radio shown the door. You could now listen to two way family favourites, Sunday lunch time and Top of the Pops on Radio Luxemburg in the evening like we have never heard it before as with the battery radio. The battery was always low at the weekend as Tuesday was the day the charged batteries came and the other ones taken for charging. I could now listen to boxing matches on the radio which I enjoyed. Bruce Woodcock, Jack Gardner, Randolf Turpin, Rocky Marciano all had their fights broadcast. Eamon Andrews commentating with W. Barrington Dolby doing inter round summaries. I think a couple more years went by before mother had a television. Father went along with all the modernisation as he was at sea most of the time and mother was in charge of home affairs. In the summer months as they do now, the council cut the grass on the roadside verges but instead of mulching it all up as they do nowadays, it was cut with a tractor mounted clipper and it made good hay so I used to gather it up for my rabbits. Mr Bush from St Michael's used to rack it up and cart it home on his pony cart. The pony would be going backwards and forwards with loads of hay from the roadsides of St Michael's, All Saints and down the road towards St James. He used to keep a few cattle and it came in handy for winter feed. I remember Mr Bush had a Red Poll house cow which used to graze on St Michael's common but it didn't have a tail. I don't know how that came about. The flies used to craze it in the summertime. Whilst on the subject of carts, me and my brother's friend Teddy Graham, he was our age, used to play together. He lived in Rose Cottage on the corner. We had a pony cart but we didn't have a pony, so one of us boys would get in the shafts and drag this cart about with one in the back. If two got in the cart he would kick up and the shafts would go up in the air. We would also use this pony cart to build our November the 5th bonfire. After school we would gather up anything that would burn from the roadside down Doony Lane; hedge trimmings, grass cuttings, load after load of the stuff. We would end up with a great big bonfire in the middle of All Saints common. We used to put a guy on top of the fire. The head of the guy was always a work of art. With permission we would get a big cattle beet (mangold wurzel) from one of Mr Newson's fields, take it round to Mrs Power at The White House and she would carve it into a head and face-paint the eyes. It really was too good to put on the fire but Mrs Power did our Guy's head for several years. She lived at The White House with her son Christopher. As it's a property with an acre or so of land they used it for market gardening. I used to go round after school and earn a few bob doing various tasks. One I will never forget is mowing the lawns. There were two at the front and one at the back and I used to set about mowing these with an Atco push

mower. I was not strong enough to push the thing up and down the lawn in the normal way. I stood on the spot and pushed it backwards and forwards, moved a bit more and done another bit. It took me ages to do the three lawns. By the time I was done I was absolutely whacked. It was a lovely picturesque garden. The previous owners the Bollingbrookes had surrounded the gardens and paths with stone walls, the ones where you have a double row of stones with soil in the middle and flowers planted in the top with what we now term as a patio to the south of the house with a sunken fish pond surrounded by more stone walls. Mr Power had a huge big greenhouse delivered for growing mainly tomatoes, it was big when erected. It reached from one side of the field to the other. Something like 50 meters or so and I had the job of painting every bit of timber with some sort of green wood preserve. I didn't mind that as I didn't have to be too fussy and not worry about making a mess and after week upon week of painting Mr Power said you had better give it a second coat. Needless to say I was fed up with painting time I had finished that lot again. One job I was itching to have a go at was rotivating. He had a big self propelled machine you only had to start it up and walk behind it as it done its job. But I never got to have a go. I seemed to get the jobs Mr Power didn't want to do; weeding the borders and tidy up figured high on jobs to do. It done me no harm, I have always liked a tidy garden. I have a leaning to flowers rather than veg. My brother is a very good vegetable gardener.

Further down the road on the corner is Rose Cottage, where our friend Ted Graham lived with his mother Dilly Graham and another lady named Clara. Mrs Graham had a habit of running out of groceries and Clara would be knocking on my mother's door, have you got such a thing as ½ lb sugar? That seemed to be the way of the world then; if you ran out you borrowed from your neighbours. Our mate Ted was a bit like me, he had a love of livestock. He kept ducks, chickens, goats, I think he even had a pig. One thing he did have was an open top Austin 7 motor car in the garage. I don't suppose it belonged to Ted but it was there and we spent hours in that, covering imaginary miles behind the wheel making engine noises. Not for the want of trying we couldn't get the engine started which with hindsight probably wasn't a bad thing. One lasting memory of Rose Cottage was the box hedges each side of the garden path. They used to smell lovely. When I was in Ted's company mischief was never far away. Two things spring to mind, Mrs Power next door used to have a friend from Bungay visit her quite regularly in her Austin 7 motor car. Me and Ted crept up to the motor car, lifted the bonnets, him one side me the other and we changed all the plug leads around. We went and hid up in the ditch not far away and waited ages for this lady to come out to her car. But our naughtiness back fired on us. The lady switched the ignition on, turned the handle, the engine started up and with a wave goodbye to Mrs Power, the lady in her car went oblivious up the road. Me and Ted looked at one another dumbfounded. Our other bit of mischief was with Ted's mum's new Hudson moped. Unbeknown to Mrs Graham, me and Ted used to get it out of the shed after dark, get it going and take turns in having a ride on it. In the beginning we just went up the road and back, but it got further and further. In the end we went up All Saints common, left at Rumburgh school, left into Rumburgh Long Lane, left to St Michael and left to All Saints common. Then it became a time trail. I was going round as fast as I dare, past Dolls Cottage, approaching St Michael, leaned into the bend and ended up on the heap of sugar beet of Mr Jordan's. I was alright, but the moped was bent about a bit. I couldn't get it going again. So I pushed it back to All Saints, me and Ted put it in the shed. Ted went indoors, I went home. We didn't spend much time together after that, we sort of drifted apart. Perhaps Mrs Graham put down some ground rules. But later in life Ted got married and emigrated. But I have learnt that he has now sadly past away.

The winter evenings were generally quiet in the village. I still had my rabbits to feed and look after when I got home from school. There used to be a film show Tuesday evenings at Rumburgh Village Hall, it would start with a short film each week about the adventures of The Scarlet Rider, followed by a main film. Again at Rumburgh Hall there would be a social evening most Saturday evenings through the winter. Local bands would feature. Us young lads and lasses would have fun running in and out of the hall messing about until we thought it was time to go home. The older people would be spending their time between the Rumburgh Buck and the Village Hall. Most of the men in the villages worked on the local farms and if so wished, would visit the local pub in the evenings. All Saints Red Lion, St Michael Jolly Farmers, Rumburgh Buck, St James White Horse. Each pub had their regulars who would be sitting in the same place every time I went in for a Vimto and a packet of crisps. Mr Dick Myhill and Mr Steward English I remember quite clearly. Dick was always on the right of the serving hatch and Steward on the right on the bench seats. Steward English would walk every evening from St Peter's to St Michael's Jolly Farmers for his pint and when the Jolly's closed he used to walk to All Saints Red Lion. When I was old enough to legally ride a motorcycle I pulled up beside Steward and asked him if he would like a lift, he was on his way to the Red Lion. His reply was I would sooner walk to London then have a lift with you. Perhaps he had heard about my involvement with the heap of sugar beet. Summertime always provided various things to do. Garden fetes, currant picking, swimming in the Waveney all accessed by bicycle. The first fete of the summer was at St Margaret's South Elmham at The Old Rectory and the one thing I remember about it was the lovely smell of the garden. A mixture of pine, box hedges and fresh cut grass. Another thing that used to go on at the same farm was currant picking. They grew several acres of black currants which the local women and children would go and help pick when the crop was ready. The women made a job of it picking from morning till night to supplement their income. Us youngsters would pick a few punnets to get a few pence for pocket money. The man worked on the farm overseeing it all was Rolly Smith. He used to live at Rumburgh. Rolly would be walking up and down the rows making sure you were not damaging the bushes and picking where he told you to. The next fete would be at Flixton at The Grange just before what is now the chicken factory. That was a bigger affair than St Margaret's fete. There would be a big marquee in the meadow full of flowers and vegetables and produce all being judged for best this, that and the other as well as looking around the gardens. In another meadow clay pigeon shooting was going on. The big thing for me was that if during the year you had got off your bike and so much as looked over the garden wall it was "what do you want, away with you". You could go along to the fete, pay your sixpence or so to get in do all the nosing about you wanted and nobody said anything to you. Then it was the turn of St Margaret's Ilketshall to have their fete. Another big marquee, flowers, veg etc. All being judged by some local Lady or Gent. Bowling for the pig was what it said, you won a pig. No doubt a runt but you won a pig. The fete ended with all the flowers and veg being auctioned off. In my days at the fete Mr Dick Monks a veterinary surgeon used to do it.

 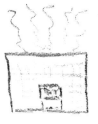

As well as the garden fetes, summer was a time we could get our body immersed in water because bathing at home was a job and a half. Mother had to boil a copper full of water. Pour it in the tin bath. After we had bathed the water had to be carried out and chucked in the ditch behind the house. It was a bit easier when the water was laid on as we had hot water at the sink. But we didn't have a bathroom. So in the summer months a gang of us village lads would cycle to Homersfield and have a swim in the River Waveney. Behind the Black Swan was the favoured spot. There would be quite a gathering of children there. The first ones down there would drive the cows out of the way. Some of us could swim to the other side, but I never ventured. I was of the thinking if I get to the other side I have to swim back. On the way back home we would stop at St Cross Fox for a Vimto and a packet of crisps. It was all Smiths Crisps in them days with a little blue twist of salt in. I had at this time got myself a job working for the Rogers at Boundary Farm St Michael. I say St Michael as I was told the boundary with St Margaret's goes through the kitchen. They used to cook in St Michael and eat in St Margaret. There were two brothers, Charles and John and two sisters Margaret and Olive Rogers. I used to work Saturdays and school holidays. Two shillings and sixpence, or half a crown as it was known, for Saturday morning (eight till twelve) or five shillings for all day Saturday (eight till half past four), in today's money twenty five pence. Several local men worked for the Rogers Brothers. Mr Billy Adnams was the full time carpenter, builder and general maintenance man. Mr Adnams also had his own workshop at his home on St Michael's common and I think he also made the gates still in use at St Michael's church. Mr Harold Head was the pig man. They kept hundreds of pigs, large white sows and Landrace boars. I can remember asking Mr Head how baby pigs running about on a meadow with dozens of others find their mothers. Same as you find your mother he said, to the pig they all look different. They also reared a lot of fat cattle and kept a large laying flock of hens up The Poplars - that was a farm one mile to the north of Boundary Farm up a long drive. The old farmhouse to The Poplars was also full of hens. The windows were netted up and the internal doors removed and the hens had the run of the place upstairs and downstairs.

 And then there was Klondyke, Mr Fred Shepherd. Klondyke lived in the council houses on All Saints common with his mother and sister, the ones facing the common. He had to cycle past our house to get to work. On his way home from work, me, my brother and sister would be playing outside. Klondyke would pull up on his bike and tell us marvellous stories about how he won the war single handed. Each time was a different story. Klondyke was a general farm worker. He would be flashing out the ditches along the side of the road in the summer and cutting hedges in winter. There's a big water course running past Boundary Farm, that's where Klondyke would be in the summer months. My duties included cleaning the car, polishing their shoes, chopping sticks. If I worked a full day I would be cleaning the silver or turning the churn making butter. I also learnt left from right working for the Rogers. One Easter holiday Charlie said "Terry I want you to go stone picking down the lane towards The Poplars in the field on the right". Well I didn't know left from right. So I had a look in both fields, they were both stony so I took pot luck and armed with a steel bucket started stone picking, putting them in heaps. It wasn't long before Charles pulled up. "Terry you are in the wrong field, I said the one on the right." That got that sorted out. Another Saturday morning job I remember well was taking the horse to the blacksmiths in Rumburgh for shoeing. She's all ready to go said Mr Rogers, you will be alright, I hope you don't meet anything to frighten the horse. I was fourteen but this horse still towered over me. So off we go me leading the horse. I was a bit nervous. Right out of Boundary Farm and right into Rumburgh Long Lane, so far so good then my heart sank into my boots. Up ahead was the worst thing I could run into. Mr Billy Colyers Field Marshall and all the threshing tackle. I must admit I was a bit scared if the horse wanted to run away. There wasn't much I could do about it. I got on the side as much as I could. Mr Colyer

slowed right down and eased past me and the horse. The old horse didn't batter an eyelid. No doubt seen it all before. I was on top of the world then. If I run into anything else it's not going to be any worse than the threshing tackle. So we clipped clopped to the blacksmiths near Rumburgh shop. I watched the horse being shod, it's a smell you never forget, hot horse shoes burning into a horses hoof. I got back to Boundary Farm in time to bike home for dinner. Miss Margaret Rogers was very strict. She would give me various jobs to do. "Terry look at me when I am talking to you, pay attention" she would bark out. It done me no harm at all, and helped to wear off some rough edges and prepare me for a working life I am now about to embark on. But before I go off to work I want to touch on two topics of what Christmas was like in the 1940s and 50s, also winter fuel. As afore mentioned, there was no electricity or water in them days. Now we sit and watch Christmas adverts on the telly in September and decorations up in November. Back then it was very different. One of the first signs of Christmas was on the way, when mother would start making two Christmas puddings October/November time. Your heart skipped a beat. Christmas is coming. Then at school, if I hadn't ran home, as in the early days we would start making Christmas cards and paper chains. Bits of paper cut into strips, a bit of sticky on one end, put it through the last hoop and stick the end up. We used to make yards of them. They all hung about the house somewhere. Mother would be going to Bungay on the bus or later on it would be Harleston. No doubt getting presents and all the other extra stuff for Christmas. Father would be on the home fishing at that time of year fishing out of Lowestoft herring catching. He would be home every Saturday night before setting sail again Sunday morning and that would be the pattern up to Christmas. He would have a week off over Christmas and then he would say cheerio Nellie, be good children, and would disappear down the road on his bike. Sail out of Lowestoft around to Milford Haven until May. He would then come home for a couple of weeks. Mother would get father to paint the house up. He didn't take long, soon got that job out of the way. He would borrow a ladder from Mr Newson across the common, get the paint out and start painting (green) take the ladder back in the evening, job done! He painted over everything, cracks, blisters, birds mess, sparrow's nesting material hanging down the facia boards, it all got painted. Another one of father's talents was puncture mending. He would come outside with a couple of mother's tablespoons, and after a lot of cursing and spoon bending would get the tyre off. He would pump the tube up. Where he thought there was one puncture there is now three. Put the patches on, pump up, put the tube in a bucket of water, all ok. After more spoon bending the tyre would be back on. Pump the tyre up. Within minutes it would be flat again, more punctures and this would carry on until he got fed up with it. He would stuff the tyre full of grass, and when his two week holiday was up and time to go back to sea, he would somehow ride his bike to Bungay and leave it at the cycle shop for Percy Harmer to sort out. Father would then get the bus to Lowestoft and sail away round to Fleetwood and then round the top of the country to North or South Shields by late September/October time. He would be home again Saturday nights fishing out of Lowestoft the very first sign of Christmas on the way. Then as Christmas got nearer Mr Sampson the greengrocer from Bungay would bring the tree on one of his regular Friday rounds. Then mother would start baking, mince pies, sausage rolls, jam tarts all manner of stuff. The Christmas cake would have already been made. Christmas carols would be crackling out of the battery radio. Mother would send us off to find some holly. There were only two holly trees in the village, one across the common in one of Mr Newson's meadows and one down St Margaret's Road near the tin buildings. Mr Newson's tree was a big old tree with the berries right at the top and the one down St Margaret's Road was a bushy old tree with only a few berries you could count on one hand. So if you had a bit of holly for Christmas you were lucky. And you knew the big day was upon us when we were told to get the bucket out of the shed and fill it up with sand from the heap on the corner, ready to put the tree in. With our paraffin lamps in hand we would be ushered off to bed, lay there listening to noise from the kitchen below and the creatures running about the ceiling above. Next morning when you woke up, one of father's white fishing socks hung on the end of our beds full of fruit, nuts and bits and pieces. Downstairs we rushed, tree up and all decorated in the front room, trimmings everywhere, presents under the tree. Tin clockwork tractors, Meccano sets, farmyard toys of all description and no doubt presents for my sister, we were all treated equally. Mother would be up and the black turkey or cockerel bought from Mr Watts at The Willows would already be in the oven. The house would be warm. She would be busy getting ready for Christmas dinner as uncles, aunts and cousins would be round for dinner and tea. We would all be in front of the fire in the front room, the only time of the year we went in there. Us children would be playing about and joining in with the parents playing snap, draughts, dominos, snakes and ladders, all sorts of games well into the evening. The next day we would do it all again around one of our uncle and aunt's house and so on till everyone had their turn. Mother used to love Christmas and always treated herself to two bottles of Stones Ginger Wine and then it was cheerio Nellie, be good children and father sailed away for another year.

One of our jobs at weekends was chopping sticks and sawing wood enough to last the week, this was done to supplement the coal. The coalman called every week delivering two bags so the heap in the shed built up in the summer and decreased in the winter. With most men working on farms there was access to sticks and wood. After Christmas hedge cutting and coppicing out woods would be done with all the sticks being tied either with string or a young twig into bundles called fagots. Most of the households had a heap of fagots in the backyard with a chopping block and bill hook for the job. Wood was carted home on horse and tumbril or tractor and trailer apart from fallen trees. Some farmers would let you stowe a tree, cut the top out, not so much oaks and ash but low growing trees to keep them in check and as mentioned earlier hedges were being pulled out, trees felled so wood became easy to get hold of. And then the electric came, with that the central heating and the fagots and heaps of wood have in some cases given way to oil tanks.

A RAMBLE THROUGH THE PAST

Farming in the forties and fifties was mostly mixed. There weren't many farms that didn't have a few cows. Mr Baker at St Micheal's Jolly Farmers had five or six on his dozen or so acres that went with the pub. The average herd size was about twenty five. Outside the farms by the road was the churn stand where the ten gallon churns would be put on ready for collection. TJ Kidner from Brampton would collect all the full ones and drop off empties, ready for the next milking. They all used to go to the dairy at Halesworth, right opposite the railway station. It used to be a feature of Halesworth station, milk churns rattling and banging. There was still a bit of hand milking going on but most farms had a Lister Stationary Engine driving a vacuum pump to operate the Gasgoine or Alpha Laval Bucket Milkers. You still see them about today at country fairs. Some of the local farmers used to keep a billy goat under the notion that the smell would ward off disease. Mr Jack Jordan used to gather up the cows afterbirth and hang it on the hedge away from the cow shed, he thought that would keep the herd free from disease. His son Roy used to say the only thing that would do, was keep the flies out of the cow shed. There would be hens for egg production, barn yard fowl and hut and run set-ups also a few cockerels to put on the shack and fatten up for Christmas. Most farms kept pigs. Saddlebacks were very popular. Essex and Wessex, Large Blacks,

Large White, Landrace Boars were introduced to Large White sows to produce a longer leaner pig; the beginnings of pig improvement schemes. Harvest time was very labour intensive. There would be someone driving the tractor pulling the binder, another sitting on the binder adjusting the height of the sails and cutter bed as it went along. Another gang shocking, that's standing the sheaths on end to let the air through, then the sheaths had to be carted to the stack yard. Horse or tractor drawn wagon, one or two people on the wagon loading ears inward. Two more pitching using a long handle two tine pitch fork. When the wagon was loaded a couple of ropes were thrown over, one at the front and one at the back. You would then set off for the stack yard. That's where I came in driving away. In the stack yard a bottom would already have been laid using bushes and old 'over a year old' straw. There would be another gang ready to unload. One on the load, putting the sheaths on the straw pitcher, one standing bully in the bully hole; he would be passing the sheaths to another one or two building the stack.

At the end of harvest the stack yard would be full of stacks ready for thatching and the amount of bits of wood propped up holding the ends of the stacks in would provide a talking point amongst the village folk. There's enough wood around that stack it will soon walk out of the stack yard. During the autumn and winter months Mr Billy Colyer would turn up with his threshing tackle, Field Marshall tractor, drum and straw pitcher, sometimes a stationary baler. This would all be stood in order against the stack. Anyone in the village who could give a hand was asked to help with this job. You needed a lot of people.

Three on the corn stack with one standing bully passing the sheaths to the man on the drum cutting the bonds (string). Probably three on the straw stack after the straw has gone through the drum, two or three bagging the corn and one bagging chaff. Anything up to a dozen people. There is a thirty six foot cut Claas combine working across the fields with another chap driving a tractor and corn trailer. It takes just two people from field to grain store, how things have changed in sixty years.

Although very few people had a motor car. The villages were well provided for. St Margaret South Elmham, St Margarets Ilkitshall, St Michael, St James, Rumburgh all had a shop, also a tradesman called most days of the week; butcher, baker, hardware, greengrocer, groceries. Mother's grocery order came on Thursdays; Co-op from Bungay. The delivery man would come carrying a great box of groceries up the garden path and he would take another order book away with him for next week. As well as the regular callers you also had men selling out of suitcases; various clothing, silk ties, Kleen-eze. Sometimes you would get an onion seller on a bike, somebody sharpening knives, more often in the sumer months would be the ice cream van, Joe Peruzzi hot pie and peas, Lovely, Fish and chip van, the Corona soft drinks man would call house to house most weeks. There was a petrol pump at Bradley Bakers blacksmith's shop opposite Rumburgh Buck. It was a mechanical pump. He would fill up his gallon measures and then pour it into what or whoever needs it. PC Day was the village policeman, he lived in the police house in St Margaret's South Elmham. You used to see him about on his bike most days. I don't know what he had to do as I cannot remember any crime. Perhaps I wasn't old enough to know. All I have is fond memories of growing up in The Saints.

Terry Aldous

I would like to thank the staff of Leiston Press for the help and guidance in compiling this book, with special thanks to Penny Smith.